Beasts Behave in Foreign Land

Beasts Behave in Foreign Land

poems

Ruth Irupé Sanabria

Red Hen Press | *Pasadena, CA*

Book layout by Sarah Wong & Selena Trager

Library of Congress Cataloging-in-Publication Data
Names: Sanabria, Ruth Irupé, 1975– author.
Title: Beasts behave in foreign land / poems Ruth Irupé Sanabria.
Description: First edition. | Pasadena, Ca : Red Hen Press, [2017]
Identifiers: LCCN 2016048414 (print) | LCCN 2017002525 (ebook) | ISBN
  9781597097635 (pbk. : alk. paper) | ISBN 9781597095778 (EBook)
Classification: LCC PS3619.A487 A6 2017 (print) | LCC PS3619.A487 (ebook) |
  DDC 811/.6—dc23
LC record available at https://lccn.loc.gov/2016048414

The National Endowment for the Arts, the Los Angeles County Arts Commission, the
Dwight Stuart Youth Foundation, the Max Factor Family Foundation, the Pasadena Tour-
nament of Roses Foundation, the Pasadena Arts & Culture Commission and the City of
Pasadena Cultural Affairs Division, the City of Los Angeles Department of Cultural Affairs,
the Audrey & Sydney Irmas Charitable Foundation, Sony Pictures Entertainment, Amazon
Literary Partnership, and the Sherwood Foundation partially support Red Hen Press.

First Edition
Published by Red Hen Press
www.redhen.org

Acknowledgments

Thank you Lorna Dee Cervantes. Without your belief and guidance, this book would not be possible.

Thank you to the many hardworking and dedicated people at Red Hen Press who assisted in the creation of this book and to University of Notre Dame's Institute for Latino Studies/ Letras Latinas, and especially to Francisco Aragón for opening doors and creating opportunities for Latina and Latino writers at different stages in their careers. I am honored and grateful to participate in this amazing literary movement.

Jennifer Browdy, Elizabeth Cohn, Annette Levine, Linn Shapiro, and Nicole Caso, thank you for creating spaces and bridges to share my work.

Isai, Eva, Anahi, Carlos, Cristi, Antonio, Chino, Kati, Maritza, Lidia, Luis, Kristin, Tupi, Ysabel Y. Gonzalez, Aracelis Girmay, Elizabeth Alexander, Ellen Hagan, Gail Wronsky, Lauren Marie Schmidt, Margaret Randall, Marie Howe, Martín Espada, Rich Villar, Richard Kearns, Tyehimba Jess, Randall Horton, Sarah Browning, Sarah Kain Gutowski, and Sharon Olds— whether you know it or not, you gave me insight, courage, and fuel during one, many, or all stages of creating these poems—thank you.

Raquel y Alicia thank you for sharing life, canvas, microphone, and page with me, honestly and courageously.

Acknowledgment is gratefully given to the following publications in which some of these poems originally appeared: *Writing Fire: An Anthology Celebrating the Power of Women's Words* and *Long Dumb Voices: A Poetry Review*, http://www.longdumbvoices.org/.

For all my tías, tíos, mothers, fathers, guides, and voices *presentes, ahora y siempre.*

Contents

II

Introduction

Open this book:

> *And with good luck, we will swim*
> *in the pool of a human being's memory.*
> —"Latin American Women Write In Exile"

We, the "offspring's offspring / who are telling a story" are in these pages; in this case, one of what another will not do to another human being. Here are profusely beautiful, startlingly savage and achingly lyrical docupoems wrought and rendered from one human being's memory.

Ruth Irupé Sanabria's poems are not so much political as they are providing the bodies to witness from four generations of females—as evidence that "the political is personal" by unravelling the facts and effects of political foreign policy upon a single family and rippling out. Beasts behave as beasts will do in a foreign land, as they do here across our American geo-political borders.

This is a poetry that sings itself whole, as Walt Whitman sang a song of Self —"for I, too, am America"—that mass of humanity here in this time. This is a poetry of detail and Truth as only a Latina living in US exile can present it. Each poem attests to its own individuality, voice and craft. There is no one style or school of poetry in this book. There is the truth of the poem and the "minute particulars" of experience, some carved out of documents of witness and trial. These well-crafted poems testify as much as they enchant. This is a poetry of survival and grace; each poem, a single strategy; every word, another witness.

Part prayer. Part testimony. All heart. *Beasts Behave* refuses to lie down and be quiet, refuses to compromise beauty or the beast: the beast we carry within, the one forged in us through multiple denials. This book, with its confident and competent voice and diverse ways of seeing, leads us into and out of the labyrinth of the self and the labyrinths of history—presents Herstory with its torture and song. This book sings. This book tells the truth, the truth of "our vacuous beginning on the highway / and the big inevitable bang."

—Lorna Dee Cervantes
November, 2016
Olympia, WA

I

The Collapse of Greta Oto, the Transparent Revolutionary Butterfly

The EMT administered as much salvia as he thought her body could process
but she kept driveling on about salvation and memory.

Earlier that week a concerned citizen had snitched.
The report read that she was ruining the landscape with her limp-winged hobble.
No one could ask her about her day; she kept yammering,
"Some confuse salvation and saving souls
with managing the massive emptiness in the yards.
Memory is spayed.
Nothing flowers robust and sweet."

She had been captured easily.

Like all minds that surrender, she had always struggled with her proclivity
to be limp-winged but had managed it well until the day she sunk
into an editorial reveling in the recent death of her mother
and condemning her mother's *compañeros* for revering "the 'fire of subversion,'
the way deer venerate the sweet, dark-pink flesh
and smooth, sturdy canes of a thorn-less raspberry bush.
When the Beast of Memory spews his fire, may they all burn!"

Now, strapped down to the stretcher, spiracle mask fogging up,
there was no point in holding back truth when the Admitting Chair asked
what she thought about fire, so she confessed: her heart feared
the transmutation of an era into a fragment of a puzzle.

"It says in your chart that your first and only mission
through the Throat of Silence landed you here,"
the Admitting Chair mumbled while checking the strength of her thorax.
"Mining Memory's Throat is a solitary practice, only in theory,"
he whispered so as to not be overheard, then closed the chart and scuttled away.

A window came in and placed an extra blanket on her bed. "Here, just in case."

"Window," she called out, "My caterpillars? The fire? The Beast of Memory?"

The window upped the oxygen, leaned in, "Breathe up.
You've got to abandon that 'work.' With wings as transparent as yours,
you have no business mining Memory's Throat.
Who's going to pull you from the long silence next time?"

"But, my babies. Did they make it?"

"You need to sort your realities if you want to get out of here."

Mother's Milk

Attach to me like a wiggling piglet.
Suckle, and suckle, and suckle.
I have not killed a hen,
much less walked to the butcher
since the doctor pulled you out and onto me.

Like a parenthesis trying to form an O, your legs stay bowed.
Son, slow animals are killed in a flash.

Doctors prescribe the sun
to calcify you straight.
Here, my piglet, my nipples dry themselves out.
Ordinary cow's milk will not do.
A bit of warm brandy in your bottle
for the battle you'll walk.

And now, for the battle you'll walk
I will turn my back to you.
Listen. These are my hands and this is the sound
of straight bones and strings bending to my intention.
If sun and brandy won't heal you,
son, music will.

Seconds before Giving Her Testimony, the Witness Requests a Glass of Water to Quell the Voices Planted in Her on the Day the Soldiers Came for Her Family

"Begin with: *this is the only picture I have of the three of us together.*"

"Put that away! The carrion needs to rest."

"Don't be a pussy. Look at the photo."

"Now that's that face of a mother who would rather be anywhere else but at her daughter's first birthday."

"Do you even know the names of the soldiers on trial?"

"Your mother shaved her legs and wore a dress that day."

"Don't mention your father. For his sake."

"Tell the judges how mirrors grow down your mother's spine; how her neck is the long bending neck of an old adolescent, a new mother, a narcissist."

"Don't be a self-absorbed cunt. Focus on the grenades, the helicopters, and the moment of kidnapping. Keep the mommy issues for your bourbon."

"How do you say 'Your Honor' in Spanish?"

"Since we're on the topic of honesty, you should mention that your mother never loved your father like that. She needed him. To get out of her father's house. Sadly, she got knocked up on her honeymoon."

"First of all, no one wants to hear how you two are as warm and fuzzy with each other as a pair of frozen steaks. Even if it is relevant to the case."

"And squeeze as much eloquence as you can from your Spanish."

"Your mother braided all of her resilience into your umbilical helix of breath and
memory. You'll do fine."

"Focus: the flashbacks, the exile, the silence."

"Bleh. The skeletons are on parade. Again."

"Testifying validates the historical and political significance of the individual's
experience. However, in trials like these, for crimes against humanity perpetrated by
military forces against its own citizenry, an insular approach to understanding one's
narrative in which one delineates her testimony from the collective 'I' as critically
important is problematic. The witness knows that once her turn on the stand is
through, what she has offered will be absorbed into a larger, stronger mass that will
outlive her. The witness has betrayed the nacreous silence, which, for decades, she
labored over. She might feel disoriented, even embarrassed, by the sudden release and
exposure of what obsessed and defined her most."

"What the fuck?"

"*Hasta la muerte, camarada.*"

"The Judges are listening. Speak."

Ars Poetica

Story takes her skin. Story takes her bones.
She finds her toes and her fingertips.
When she speaks, like salmon running,
the dead and the living converge.
The river of memory rocks
the hunger of claws and tongues.
Electricity swallows itself back
through its double-prod *picana,*
bullets dislodge themselves from
their chore of destroying
the same day over and over again,
and from the caverns of fear and revision,
skin resurrects the skin.
Each sentence closes in
like the crawl of split skin
sealing its red, wet avulsion.

The enormity of the pending night scares the seven assassins on trial.
They understand that in hell, they will eat their own throats.

Mother, Daughter, Soldier, Ten Ants, and One Turtle: An Intertextual Fable/Testimony in Translation[1]

Ten little ants marched up and said:

The doorbell rang incessantly.

"Good turtle, if you give us just one little leaf of your juicy lettuce."

I rushed to answer the door, my daughter close behind, when suddenly we heard

"Just one leaf and we'll tell you a story."

men banging the door and yelling, "Army! Open the door!"

"It's a deal!" replied the curious little turtle.

I turned and ran. For a second, I consider taking her with me and jumping over the hedge at the back of our house.

And so, the ten little ants carried away their juicy leaf of lettuce.

Instead, I kissed her. Then, I ran and jumped. My daughter broke into a wail. That's the last I knew of her.

Meanwhile, Juanita the Turtle waited impatiently for their return.

I heard a bullet, I heard shots fired, and I didn't know what had happened to her.

A few minutes later, the ten little ants returned and this is the story they told:

---

1 Composed with a story written to me by my mother while she was a political prisoner and with adaptations of my testimony and those belonging to my mother and to a former soldier who testified in the Trials against the Fifth Army Corps in Bahía Blanca, Argentina.

That day, I was playing in the courtyard when suddenly I heard a loud banging at the door.

"Tucked away in a little nook in Mr. Pemperlin's garden, Juanita the Turtle munched on a head of lettuce."

My mother picks me up, runs inside, and leaves me on her bed. I hear men shouting and I see my mother leaving me.

"When ten little ants marched up to her and said: 'Little Turtle, if you give us one leaf of that juicy lettuce.

They had kidnapped a mother and abandoned her child.

Just one leaf—

I walked into the apartment on the sergeant's orders. He handed me some papers he'd found. That's when I saw the little girl on the bed, crying.

we will tell you a story ...'

A few moments later, they caught the mother, and with the assistance of a soldier, managed to shove her in.

"It's a deal!" replied the curious little turtle.

I asked the sergeant what they planned to do with the little girl.

And that's how, by losing one leaf of her juicy lettuce,

The sergeant replied they'd arranged to leave the child with some neighbors.

Juanita the Turtle learned

For many years later, this experience troubled me. The little girl haunted my dreams. Not knowing her fate and if her mother was dead scarred me.

That it's bad to be so curious.

Landfall

The segue is without warning
from a fatherly lesson on the food of the gods,
and the ritual killing that contented them
to the story of an old college classmate,
who in '76 was found hanging upside down
from a bridge, balls stuffed in his mouth,
lips sewn shut. The military did it.

You resume the lesson chocolate.

Chocolate dragées sink and disappear,
whipped cream implodes,
and all the sugar undoes itself in the liquid heat.

I attempt a flashback of my own:
back when you were in prison,
abuelo would sit me in a row of men and their coffee.
I'd spin on the red swivel stool; the world was steel in and out
until the white demitasse of steaming milk appeared
and I'd unpeel the silver wrapper off the semisweet bar
and dunk it, and let it sink and dissolve, tragic submarine,
delicious in the end.

I lose this round.
Flashback is to memory what raptor is to bird.
I order cake to balance out the drink of bitter gods.

The Cardinal Delivers Us

Baptize the cardinal in our yard
when I ask: *where is my mother?*

When I ask: *where is my mother?*
marvel at the cardinal you've named

for she flew to us
an ember among the ovenbirds.

What truths can a cardinal sing?
A bird knows a bird's song
attracts its own fate, not ours.

We are a swirl of red feathers on a canvas.
We are a scarlet flutter in a poem.

I'd climb the almond tree,
climb the brick wall,
and follow the cat
to learn how the cat finishes the cardinal.

Undone by the Shadows
(Four Variations on the Same)
After *Abrumados por las Sombras*, painting by Raquel Partnoy

1.
Hold. Hold. Hold this pose. This pose: husband/wife
& this third thing. This third child, our daughter's
shadow, marooned between us; the condor's
green army truck tarp sinks. We've sunk our daughter.
I can't find her in this third child. Pull! Pull
out my old dolls. Let her play while we breathe.

2.
I'm the one who set my young daughter under my easel
while I worked light into the dancing tamarisks.
I chose to drown myself and to revive
from the ravel of vines and dried flowers—
burn *me* instead. *I* taught *her* to coax oxygen from darkness.
Where she is, she is breathing through these oils.

3.
Run! This theater devours our daughter.
Whiskey-drive to the edge of our red city.
Drive faster than horses break earth. Find her.
Locked warehouses and open sky Pampas, windmills and creeks,
sidewalks, and downcast eyes—defy them. They all know. They all saw.
Come home with her or stay gone!

4.
Who you've loved along the way, abandon.
Come back to this mess . . . this plate of fried brain waits
for you and the nothing you bring home.
Did we ever teach her the acrobatics of fear,
how to walk the tightrope of solitude?

Beasts Behave in Foreign Land

Up the slug-filled hill,
around privacy trees and hedges,
through cracks in the imperfect,
swollen door and thin glass windows
of a rented blue house, the yellow lions roar.
I'll give my guardian an anonymous name and testify:
those lions at the zoo down the hill and this uncle of mine are the same—
hunted, captured, encaged. Now look, good world.

The hoods, the bars,
the whips, the prods
will follow beasts through water and flight.
The hoods, the bars,
the whips, the prods
make beasts do their best to turn life into lead,
though papers say:
beast, you are freed,
beast, you are rescued,
beast, walk in the freedom.

No beast heals in a blue house
listening to another beast roar all morning long.

One remedy is to talk to beer
and to the recording of a song
in search of *mi unicornio azul.*
No, not in search of a *lost* unicorn,
but of *my* blue unicorn, disappeared and gone.

A yellow fire rings itself around my shiny black shoes.
I jump o-o-over the rising hot rings—roars around my feet.

Our golden Tango, roped to his blue doghouse, lunges out.
I watch my guardian and his beer and his song.
Our dog is choked back into his house.
The lion, a hill away, burns.

I know the beast is mean if I, if I . . .

But men can build the cage and watch,
and men can eat pink sugar and drool.
And I know what rage that thing would have
if that thing were free.

We would not run with gratitude if released.

Lap of Crows

After *El Regazo de los Cuervos*, painting by Raquel Partnoy

In the violent valleys of the Testaments,
women dance! The bride spins beheaded;
her groom nestles into her perfumed neck.
Dance returns and returns between the mourning

mountains of the remains: infirmed and drunk.
Without scorecards and roses, women dance.
And amidst the canvasses of this dance,
one will sit, amber eyes alit, breasts not yet chewed.

Blood lariat bedecking her décolletage,
hands crossed on her pregnant lap of crows,
womb thick with jonquil, carmine, and indigo feathers.
One crow walks her shoulder with prophecy.

Raise crows and they'll pluck your eyes out.
But she sees, she sees.

Refugees in the Attic on Lamont Street

We are the resident ghosts,
atheist in the blue dollhouse.

Our hosts are white and subversive
and devoted to Jesus.

I descend from their attic.
I want their mints and their chocolate bunnies.
God will punish me
if I steal.

How to not bend in confusion
or in desperate gratitude,
how to not be too quiet when seen,
how to listen to their language, befriend their words—
these things my mother shows me.

To rebuild my body,
I watch her build her own.
I spin alone in the quiet attic room.
I spy on raccoons from the edges of the attic window.
I float back across the sky.

Yes, the walls warm.
Yes, the floors hold.
Their roof is stable, yes.

Without scandalous sounds
they raise their wineglasses to us.

They break bread with us.
We hold our tongues.

We drop our heads
for grace.

Distance

My grandfather asked me: could I remember
him, the park, the birds, the bread?
I'll be dying soon, he said.

His voice would stretch the ocean and end there,
inside the olive phone in our tiny kitchen.
My mother would stretch the green shell to my ear,
speak, say something, speak. My fingers tugged the cord
across our red wooden table. Listening to the dark adios,
I carved half moons into the wood with my fingernails.
In case I am dead by your next birthday, hija, *remember . . .*

We ate without him, without any elders
and the world was fine.

We have yet to bury our bones in this foreign land.
When we do, where will we come from then?
Already, *home* is a carnation pinned to our cold breasts.

Hiking with My Father

On the lookout for bears, cougars, hypothermia,
starvation, poisonous bugs, trees falling, landslides,
avalanches, poisonous berries, snakes, frostbite,
cuts, sprains, dehydration, and Confederate flags,
through Snoqualmie Falls, the Olympic Mountains,
and finally, Mount St. Helens,
we now witness
patches of miniscule purple petals
blooming so soon after the blast,
blooming from the sterile dust,
blooming from the forest of the standing dead.

We lean forward in the railings
towards the burnt saint
and her new fringe of purple lupine.

Notice, dad, the Saint's scars
and her new patterns
of moving water,
of receiving water,
of sharing water.
This is how it is to adapt
to lack of air, to loss of earth,
and to a cooler sun.

Where is the well of courage
or is it madness to rise again at the rim of violence?

Midnight Convergence on the Ravaged Heart

Heart, I've confused you with a tambourine again.
Shake in, shake in life, life, come, come life, come, *corazon*.
An exodus echoes through the rooms of this violet streaked brain.

I am a lonely daughter tonight.
There is an exodus in this house.

The water boils. The water bubbles.
Come see my angels.

Come play with the angels I've made for the blue sea.
Come have tea.
Invite me, clearly, home this year.

Oh *mamá*, this rose is a rock.
The rock in your hand is the rock from the ground.
And headless uncles gallop through my rooms
claiming we don't love them, we don't love them anymore.

They don't stop, these potlucks for the dead.
Call and keep me, and take what you called for.
The moon is a cold rock above.
Heads find their barbed wire spines before dawn.

Latin American Women Writing in Exile

"You Can't Drown the Fire. That's stupid!"
The gas station attendant spat and pumped our gas.

The poet I most admired at that time,
my father's girlfriend, spoke back,
"Her mother edited this book!"

The gas station attendant kept pumping.
I was the only other person in the car.
He waited for me.

My mother's book of embers,
its cover, *Frida's Self Portrait II*, smoldered
in my hands; my face incandesced.

"I don't care who her mother is,
you *can* drown the fire."

"You're going to let him say that?"

The worst part of that minute was
that the car had no air conditioning
and he had the basis of a philosophical argument:
water makes us and beats us.

Our most fetid fluids coax life to come again
and quiet our inexhaustible loneliness.
Then, we disappear.

And with good luck, we will swim
in the pool of a human being's memory.

We will travel down a sad cheek,
kiss it and kiss it
before evanescing. We will become
fog on another's windows.
We will morph
into this morning's breathtaking dew,
into the unforeseen
drizzles and downpours; we will reincarnate
in the wet breath of the offspring's offspring
who is telling a story.

Because I Hate Standing Still and Waiting in the Dark

I drag my feet through the leaves and sticks.
    I ignore midnight's warning
about the pieces of women found beneath leaves.
    I am equally afraid of sitting
at night on a bench in a transparent cubicle
    lit by an orange streetlamp with a schedule posted on it
listing when the next rolling box will come for me,
    while cars slow down to look at me and I cannot see
if soundless feet encircle me in all that open, stripped night.
    Tonight, I'd rather walk
alone through the moonlit woods, moving towards home on my own feet
    than wait for civilization to arrive;
I'll walk through maples, oaks, firs
    without whistle, cell phone,
    knife, blade, mace;
    without my heart avalanching in fear.
The owl flashes her yellow eyes.
The moon plays with her veils.
The possum hisses his last defense.
I smell the differences between the trees.
I allow the wind to rope around my neck.

Ruby

After *Rubí*, painting by Raquel Partnoy

1.

We're supposed to be out there on the sofa but
now she's gone through this lady's fuck-clothes,
lipstick, and whatnot. And she's in the fuck-mirror high as hell,
eyes halved, hand hipped, head titled back, and blowing
fuchsia kisses; her kisses ricocheting mirror me her mirror me her.
"Take a picture for my grandma," she smiles
wearing this lady's black negligee. Her tits want me
to suck them or rip her out of that lace.

2.

The painter goes scarlet on scarlet for this one.
This girl's problem: her whole story is a problem.
Her tongue and lifeline suffer from reticence.
The wreckage alights on oxygen's vivid mouth and sucks.

3.

Smack about nasty bitches she's gonna beat floats like blown out dandelion seed
puffs into the coke mirror of her mangled story. The painter blurs the girl's face.

4.

"You are a very angry young woman!" hisses the Dean of Students.
"Do you even like Americans? Sounds like you hate us," alleges the man in the audience.

"No. No. No," pleads the girl, "It's that I've never been good with the needle and thread
of words."

"No. No. No," pleads the girl, "It's that I've never been good at capturing the nuances of
Bambi's mother getting shot."

5.
The painter knows that her subject knows love's deadlines, will mock them both.
Neither are prone to light laughter. Distance, the white-suited, headless pimp holding
a stack of undelivered mail in his pink hands, will smother them both.

6.
"You just need to know how to crack a cunt in the right place,"
says the torturer handing the ink and stamp to the secretary
in charge of censuring and withholding the letters
written by the caged mothers to their children.

The Small Parts Still Left

Angels wait on an unmade bed.

In the dust
and in the grease-
grimed gift box
in the back of the cabinet
above the stove,
two heart-stemmed wedding flutes wait.

Stoic babies,
brides, and widows wait
in the attic
wearing their sepia tulles.

Glossy and matte-finished teenagers
pose high on ledges and cars.

Dolls wait
in holding cells
at the bottom of staircases,
in shoeboxes, and on altars
on their journey
to garbage bins.

Books climb books
whispering
echoes have no warranty.

Baby monitors wait in basements
to catch the sound of breath.

Mourning Doves

Daughter, flammable ropes
bind flags to their poles. Draw sun, draw star,
still bones are cast as dust.

I won't be the patriot who ignites the tires,
who beats the *bombo* while comrades clap,
who spray paints the questions without a mask.

I must find home in each bastard leaf.
Wake, daughter, and learn to leave.
Our story is made of a walking mud.

The lone sun animates the waves and wings.
Wake, daughter, day breaks.
The moon is gone. Birds sing.

Dinners

It's a bacchanal of eyes bulging, of feces and fleas, of death inflammations, of voices in the head, and I'm watching your guest eat it all up. *Salud!* Amen and hush, the madness is talking.

How can you eat like that? I ask.

You pause mid-mastication.

With electric prods on your balls and in your mouth?
How can you eat and talk like that?

I'm satisfied with my violence. I don't believe the guest's kindness.

Eat like a human being, I want to add but offer the mercy of a silenced tongue.

Carne

I've eaten pork
from *pernil* to *chuletas* to chitterlings.
I've dipped my hands in oily paper bags
of deep-fried gizzards and chicken hearts.

I've swallowed raw clams and oysters.
I've eaten a stack of jellyfish, cubes of crocodile.

I've eaten pigeon and sparrow.
I've eaten bad chicken.

I've swallowed the shiny, salty, slimy
pink and pitch caviar out of tiny Russian tins.
I've eaten goat, bull balls, and ox, and
catfish, swordfish, monkfish, and salmon.

I've eaten prawns and slopped blood stew
and I have eaten red meat
shredded, cubed, ground,
boiled, fried, broiled,
tough, tender, young, and old,
pounded, breaded, or wrapped
in dough, in phyllo, in tortilla,
nestled in the mashed
potato, *plátano*, cornmeal, or cornhusk.
Tongue in marinade,
brain burger patty, and
barbecued intestines.

I grew up with blood on my bread. *El Juguito.*
The cow's little juice reserved for the growing child.

The scent of the steak on the skillet
drew me to my mother when hungry.

Periodically, I turn.
I refuse to take in flesh.
A meal, a day, or even years I go without.
When I first felt the rejection in my nine-year-old body,
my mother bought me a shirt to honor my conscience,
pink with happy farm animals drawn in blue,
"I don't eat my friends" written across my young belly.

Victory Is Ours

Thirty-three years of this oceanic exile and in one tap you make landfall on my ruined courage.

You:

- To shove my mother into the truck was a surprising struggle.
- She was tiny, almost naked.
- You didn't touch her because you held the truck door open.
- You marveled at her physical strength.
- You didn't touch her but your partner did.
- When he took his hands off my mother, he thought it was funny: "I got her hair on my hands!"
- But she defended herself very well.
- She kept yelling.
- She kept yelling through the truck windows.
- She kept yelling that her baby was in the apartment.
- She kept yelling that her parents were coming to rescue her baby.
- She kept yelling.

?

?

And who didn't?

The fog lifts. You message me "Are you her little girl?"
On your page, you smile, arm in arm with your own two girls.
What power is this? I rub my pregnant belly.
I want to testify, but instead I *like, like, like*
and in this oblivion, manage a signal back
to someone else, *fuerza, hermanas,* then I hold you
there, eye to eye. My smartphone's blue flame in my hand—
I lay on my left side to encourage the blood flow
from my vena cava to my daughter.

Lunchbox Note #1

"You and I are safe." I keep those words to myself in a locket I hang inside my throat.

In the galaxy of our memories are forests filled with hunters. In the galaxy of our memories, ink sticks and moons, halved and holed, document the tourniquets of delirium. I don't want the poison of revolving memories on you.

First, the sun lacerates the sky into opal, opens all the animal eyes, and arches across your jogging path. The doe and her fawn wonder what danger is the human running.

Guilt leaves behind a bedazzling trail dissolved with simple table salt. I will keep the tragedies, old and book-bound on the top shelf. Pull down the words if you need history. Administer the stories yourself. I retract the terrible. Into your warm palms I drop the little silver anchor of imagination. I release you from heirlooms. I throw out the family lexicon on the suffering. Forget how children knew their mothers.

Lunchbox Note #2

Then, there is, aside from the hairy body, the canvas we walk in—the triptych we keep retouching. The first one, others point out to us, is huge and outdoing the other two.

I gesso your first canvas. That is one thing a mother can do. Or she can focus just on the frame and the proper stretching and stapling. Or she can leave it all alone.

But stop running. Stop running down the cracked-up sidewalk. And look up at the orange-eyed waking.

The dumpster filled with pounds and pounds of pork bone, *plátano* peels, and rotting rice isn't your name. The bread I want to break with you has nothing to do with the worst-thing-that-ever-happened-to-x, y, & z. No. If a remnant of now burrows forever into your nervous system, may it be a knack for distinguishing the *hoo-hoo* of a mourning dove from that of a flying tiger.

I'm looking for my keys. I'm prepping your canvas. I distinguish ricochet from tire pop, printer from machine gun, door slam from door break, but not easily. About estrangement and survival sharing space during the pockets of day, I want you to know nothing. We need to keep our oils separated. To each her hue while we swallow in the morning's pink light.

The ocean is hungry. The moon is a dot of light rising from the thick fog, turning back to look at us once more between two trees before she disappears. We are porous bags of salt water walking away.

The Unraveling

1.
I argue with my imagination at the self-help section.
I bite my lips still but my eyebrows betray me.
My heart stomps a mean *malambo*.
Customers buy their help or return it to the shelf.

I pick out a book on living with procrastination,
but my imagination yanks it from me.
Though I am safe and in the mall
here comes the past all fecund
hurling that I should have died,
that I am being watched,
and that I am a lazy girl on vacation when there is war.

Between the legs of time my future will dangle
until I learn how to cut with a swift hand.
Aside from the predicament my body is in,
the heavier condition is discovering
my autobiography in my head over and over again,
each time new and surprising, but only to myself.

There is evidence in the papyrus:
women wrecked their fetuses ages before Eve was written.
I am not in the self-help section of the bookstore at Menlo Park Mall.
I lay in a darkening room. The doctor is here.

The only window opens to a long brick back,
a mother's back. I know the sky is the exit.
And the sun is a doorknob, God's hot flower.

2.
I stopped my eyes on a starling.
His gold-flecked back, an oil spill.
A slow, thick respiration, the ravel of larval lace fed into him.
I did not pick him up; he looked exactly right
on my neighbor's sidewalk, held down by the weight of his back.

Out back, in my first garden, poppies bloomed
and my nine sunflowers took one foot up
then fell back flat—a red circle to which the bees did not come.
I did not collect them from their broken backs.

Into such, such a doubled red, too, that June, I fell
until the oxygen mask brought me back.
Were I a bird or bee, I would have flown with you.
Do you hear me, honeybee, pretty bird, baby?

3.

You fit in the gaps of my teeth like a strawberry seed, like blueberry skin. No one knows what I've eaten. But they know I haven't cared correctly for the morning and the feeding. What else have I neglected? Look at my children's teeth.

Overhead, helicopters mock us. My little sugar skull. Where my mind slips to, it will slip again. Sweet little *calavera*, so easily the charcoaled edges of one soldier and another soldier blur. It's a thumb rub of difference. Today is twenty-two years ago. I forget to tie my shoes and brush my teeth. Pink plus sign, the promise: yes. O cryptic urine, I can make the dead live again. Return, baby, forgiving and seeking love.

Sugar, understand me. The devil and his militia are coming. They will drag us to the camps where the windmills grow. Someone opened my mail. I need to find a payphone to call your father. When the time comes, we run from the machine gun soldiers on the street, the double-tongued silence on the skin, and the man looking down. He is the note-taker. And the repudiation of war and the end to war and the no war and the good people rising and what decade did I am I where is my father? The smell of burning flesh rides the Raritan while you grow inside me. Have you? Have you? Have you? Seen, seen this, my child, my baby, my son? I I I should run. I will be pulled from you. You and I will be destroyed. In a camp by a man just doing his job, just doing his job or in the final collapse and don't condescend me I know what day it is no don't condescend me. I I *I* killed you.

What Loves, Leaves

1.
A generation dials, a generation
hangs up and there are the brief heavy years
of luck perplexed when generations live
together in a wasting yellow house.

Though death is not here yet, the smells change up
suddenly from fried garlic's loud sex to
broccoli's tragic boiling apart.
Patience for the years each generation
scorns the other's food.

And the walls change. Up
go the compromises: three memories
of yours can hang here but I will choose which.
What is nailed, the strongest decide.

These are the years leaves begin their fall
and beneath the mulching weight, the new takes all.

2.
They were once raw dough.
In cloth and buckets I carried them.
Now, their bones are theirs.
And now, their eyes know to search out the moon.
And their bodies soften before the sea.
And they cover their ears and holler at the gusts of deaf winds.
I could not teach them to dance and yet, they dance.

Narcissus Poeticus

Even nothing is edible
Everything feeds me

God, I am
Starving

And your mother, my love, Your mother has hardened.

Her soul is made of stone . . .

—A. Partnoy "To My Daughter (Letters from Prison)"

II

The Eleventh House

In your house friendship was without apology,
milk curdling into buttermilk,
buttermilk clouding a clean drinking glass.

Who put chunks of stale buttermilk biscuits
into our buttermilk?

Do I swallow, do I chew, how do we do this
salvation?

And friendship was a wild cat trapped indoors
climbing up your walls,

unwilling to see the ceiling,
unwilling to admit the fact of the wall.

And friendship was a cat smelling the piss alley and growing desperate
for the long untamed grasses of the untouched yards,
one girl pawing another girl under her parent's loft bed, unrequited.

My new girl, her house is full of windows.
Her aqua sweater shows off her shoulder
and in the morning her breath is a sweet pineapple.

On Tuesday, she practices Beethoven
on the lime-green upright that came with her
and then she plunks out "Glamorous Life" and asks that I sing

over and over *without love, it ain't much.*
She offers hazelnut chocolate or lemon crème
by the spoon or on toast,

she never mentions how her hair is red
and in the summer our bodies pierce the water
becoming jackknives and cannonballs.

We aren't wild cats trapped.
We never drink tart milk.

Tatuaje

A spirit came down
and whispered in our drunk ears

mark your wombs with wild roses
and between beers I dreamed

that we were soldiers missing our mothers
which explains why we are seventeen

and in a tattoo parlor that smells of ships and motorcycles,
of leather and ocean, of marijuana and sad men's blood.

We each ask for a single rose
with a ribbon around the stem,

for a word, some power.
We want to be fire.

The artist changes channels.
We watch *Looney Tunes* as his needles start.

When we stop at the liquor store,
our roses, orange and violet, bleeding through the bandages,

I want to tell you that if we ever find ourselves blindfolded in a war,
or in an apple metaphor, accused of ruining it for everybody

with hunger, or knowledge,

I would not insist on how sacred is the tree or the light,
or how sacred is what moves us—

I'd become a storyteller.
And out of our inevitable estrangement
I'd make us up again and again.

Dawn in DC

Mice hear the floors tremble and they freeze,
    roaches kiss and run.
        The husky stretches out of his house and sniffs.
Three hours ago, my mother and stepfather laid down to sleep.
    We are spinning rapidly towards light.
        The eastern seaboard and her sleepers
           roll up towards the sun.
             I am coming down the stairs.

I don't see mice,
    roaches that linger will be killed,
        I ignore my dog.
I push on the Zenith and turn the knob.
    I mute the woman wearing a striped leotard
        and begin my warm-up.
    I bend and push against myself.
I step myself into a sweat;
        each landing of the feet, gentle and light.
The floorboards must not shake my mother's mattress.
The weight of my body must not shake her house. I am not a god here.

    When I have showered it all off, I gather my quarters.
    I walk outside. School starts in three hours.
    We are beneath the eye of the sun. Everything's aglow and the coffee is creeping.
No one will see me walking to Safeway.
    I enter Safeway certain that my two friends are still sleeping.
I buy three King-Size York Peppermint Patties.
In one block, I eat all three.
The streets are long and gray.
    A television crew has gathered at the corner.
    They catch me for their morning show.

Quick question about the riots yes or no. Chocolate between my teeth, my brain calculates how much must I now burn

American Telephone, 1985

1.
The world burns and all the children know
the first minute is free.

Three girls, we gather around the receiver
to hear the dark rooms of sex.

We giggle at the crippling loneliness of the grown
and imitate this breath into ears we cannot see.

Untouchable, we beg random voices for spankings and cocks.
We are sick, mean, and motherless fourth graders to invade

adults with a mockery of their disease,
to twist tight and funky their hearts.

Watcha got for me, big boy?

Our sticky fingers point.
We laugh. We hang up.

2.

We sat atop my navy blue carpet
stained with my habit of pissing
into a jar and holding the hot amber
up to the sun despite the smell
to study the tiny particles
whirling from the force of expulsion.
Downstairs, the drunks danced for the New Year.
We sat bored and disgusted until we decided
to congratulate random phone numbers
for winning a year's supply of adult diapers.
Every number we dialed rang unanswered
except one, a meek old voice who thought
we were her daughters, who thought
it was her lucky year when we told her she'd won.

3.
The green phone on my kitchen wall rings.
It is you with an offer: pizza, American pizza.

Oh messy, happy family of stretching cheese.
Oh bubbling mountains of mozzarella,
pepperoni, and mushrooms, and sausage, and pineapple,
and olives, and ham, and onions, and spinach.

To your house! Past the heaps of homeless men!
Panting, I reach you.
You sit on your stoop happy that I ran.
It's getting cold you said not about the night
and I am happy to be your friend.

Come and you walk me to the alley behind your house.
I see the box atop the trash can.
I smell the dough and cheese.
Smell it? You smile.
Yes.

In love with you, I open the flat box
and find a dead squirrel.

For the Girl Who Made Us Call Her "Big Sister"

We electric taped crab apples
to our flat nipples and exchanged
ding-a-ling and *pee-pee* for *dick* and *cock*.

Sisterly, she taught us to throw dollars onto tables,
to say *money is no object* when losing or winning.
And because one day we'd grow hair
on the toes, the knuckles, the lips,
the nose, the chin, the tits, the back,
and in the butt and girl hairiness is poverty,
she taught us to lock doors and to sprawl,
recline, and reach the wet skin with the blade.
Scared of ourselves, we shaved her back and butt
till her skin was as young as ours.

Her work was done.

The Recurring Dream of Mining Caverns with You

You and I worked inside the earth.
And down there, where lungs
and our large mouths are unsustainable,
where soil is deaf and indifferent
to our great love of water and air,
we re-created our humanness:
one to lead us all.
Like a man, you cautioned me: *stay with me*
and I needed you to keep me,
to keep me from killing,
to subdue me so my work would be done
for whoever would pay us
when we emerged once again into the sun.

Trapped and marched down, we both looked like boys;
hunger shaped our bodies. Our hunger
and the disease it was for us pained
the photographers. From atop the hills, they tried
to capture our dreams and any plot in our eyes,
but we walked forward like ants for history and laws.

The metal I struck buckled me,
broke *me*, not my arms. My arms kept pushing in.
We were seeds in the earth breaking
in need of sun. Oh God, we are thin-skinned.
The thought of light is a breaking touch.

In each dream, I go to you.
I have to leave I say.
My shoulders shake themselves into dust.
Earth swallows my sound.

And before the end, you always release me:
If you want to go, go.
But how will you know the difference
between up and down?

Lush

I am on
    concrete   a spinning crystal,
        bi-cone,
            multi-faceted,
two holes,
strung through
spinning up
    up
    the Hoboken Path steps
    up a fishy
       o yeasty
          night   exhausted.

Goodbye Manhattan.

I sparkle
    bordeaux
and
          blue
my blood
    glows
         through   my streetlamp lit skin,
stars tangle
     in my black curls,
my nipples harden
     into my candy,   I am mine.
My lips know
     every laugh
     they will chance
at the moon,
    at the flag,

                    at the waiting
                              to see
                              his plum testicles.
My roses are tattooed to my hip;
my rosed hips bend
to vomit the vodka.
                    I am puréed
                    and then lifted
                    arms in arms   three girls and I
                              giggle down
                              a stolen street.

                                        We stumble a prayer,
our thighs and breasts stretch
                    marked.
Morning is a liver, a sopped up sausage,
an indigestible pancake with a side order.
Morning is a greasy glitter, the silky vinegary inside
made ordinary, morning is the long and sober wait.

The Plan

I will throw your french fry box in the trash
and when the cafeteria empties, clean
your ketchup mountain, cheese dunes, spit lakes—
I wear my retribution plain. I do.

I will smile *silly girl* when you call me
a liar, a jerk, and a punk. Man up,
you'll say, and I'll say never, nevermore.
Denouement: pliant, sorry, soft with pain.

I, bee, stupidly sting you—Divine You!
Rise up and sharpie *blood* on my desk, wall, door—
I'm a wack excuse for a fly: buzzkill,
I've cock-blocked your commencement date.

Wounded in combat, I bow; do now (please).
Do not merely summarize: you are dismissed.

What Love Made Us

If night is a black wool cape,
then we are moths—

our hunger gives us the work
of chewing through night's manly frame.

Holes we make, we make knowing
some light will come through—

streetlamps, light bulbs, eventually eyes—
to expose us in our happiness.

God forbid the moon becomes a mothball.

Vulgar Us

La bebita gets: pink tutus, red hearts,
ladybugs, rainbows, ruffles, ice cream cones,
cherries, fairies, daisies, daddy's princess.

El bebito gets: blue, fatigue, dump truck, drum,
bicycle, tricycle, boat, ball, dog, frog,
cow, pig, horse, sheep, Tyrannosaurus rex.

With time, time will call her oldassbitch.

With time, time will call him oldassdouchebag.

Oldassbitch, do you keep your missing pairs?

Oldassdouchebag, do you keep your thinned wife beaters?

Everything, my babies, is a gift or is a chore.

When it is time to empty your closets,
bag everything you have to give,
then, wash everything that fears dying.

Desecada la delicada

Sin tu semilla estoy   seedless,

ay de mi,   woe is me.
You say   it's because

because of how we mix,
how we tie each other

to radiators with belts.

Because of the virgin
sinsemilla of my stuff,

you take me to the project trees
and lay out with blankets and beer.

I say *here* to the top level of the open-air
parking lot against the thick hard ledge,

all out, at two o'clock, between classes, *here*,
overlooking the pond where, at night, we witness the ghosts
of drowned Mabel dancing with her babies and her man.

I'll hold your hot outcomes.
This train won't stop.

What can I do with my lips for you to cuff me again?
I'll roll your blunt. I'll pour your beer.
I'll perfume your water. And the skin behind your ears.
I will   I will   when   (God!).

Crush me into your Dutch.
It's my fault, the crack in your weed—
too much bitch in my pot of *verduras*.
Everything's gone wrong. I don't fit in on your stoop.
Your fist opens. You drop me. My lips did so much.
My cab is here.

Along the Edge

Noisy, noisy and not a sound, I go
to the bay to release the violence of a message—
Do you remember me? Is this you I've found again?

Along the edge of Staten Island
I watch her tiny words float and drown.
The clouds dip. Gray swoops down.

Fewer birds, fewer bees, less heat; gems
dangle and dazzle from trees in this august drip
of lessening light. We are jealous and irreversibly timed.

I go to the bay to witness clouds swaddle the sun,
to witness heaven make miles
of open-beaked water. *Feed us, feed us.*

I mime the moon and swell with water and son.
In myth, a mother dies so that her son, a god will catch and let fly.
We pray to become humans with wings.

Never speak to me again
as if I am your man.
There are fewer birds in the sky, more drought
and floods. And palms coming together, come apart.

We know we must not wait
to be disposed of by what we begat.

Love Like a Militant

Bee, your workhouse falls under Pluto's light.
Pluto has gone underground.

The essential networks of helper friends
and revolutionary queen bees fail.

Bee, you have landed on the bluest blooms.
The purple erections of the butterfly bush unfurl
for the monarch's, not the worker's, curled tongue.

The colony despises you; uncool
hills of Echinacea won't put out their medicine.
Honey isn't made in the bellies of estranged bees.

The Way to It

Older than all gods: hunger.
    "I am hungry," he said.
"Here," she replied, "eat this."

I was smoking cloves
    and drinking rum.
You were hungry.

No, this is how our story begins:
    I ask you to help me
understand the Old Testament.
    I do not eat pork.
My roommate orders pepperoni pizza.
    You are hungry and polite.
Unless I eat, you won't.
    I chew the pork. Now, do you like me?
You are full, suddenly shy.

This is how it really began:
    you ask me to help you
study for a course on feminism.
    I am not hungry.
I smell of grapefruit and honey.
    You say "your fragrance is lovely."
You insist I eat:
    a corn muffin and apple juice.
    You watch me chew. Soon, I am feeding you.

This is it:
    you offer me candy,
Besitos de Coco

from Puerto Rico;
I buy you an Oatmeal Stout from Harvest Moon.
You say you want me for your life.

Exit 9

We down this galaxy of headlights
lassoed with bands and diamonds.

Our happy nerves fizzle the wild buzzing
of the million stars zooming after us southbound.

Slow this ship. Speed this ship.
Slower. Gods radar our speed.

We are blurry but able to see the signs that matter:
EXIT, EXIT, EXIT.

Patron Saint of the Commute,
your chemical flames burn twenty-four hours.
I light this votive between my lips,
drop a prayer for far-out love,
and for the honeyed moon.
O burning towers and tanks,
despite our twists in the genomes,
and thousands of years of love in the human song—
we savage this world to dust.
Bless the heat that keeps us coming together.

We could die right here, spin to death.
I could.
They would test our blood.
They would burn our bones.
And our love?

Our vacuous beginning on the highway
and the big inevitable bang

building, building
in us, makes us
slow down.
Exit here.

Amazonas

This is what I want you to eat.
This rock. This rock is gelatin.
This rock is gravel.
This rock is fruit and lizard.

This rock is bought on the side of the road
in small bags on small branches still breathing
the whole snaky way. Our tongues are satin ropes.
The car is the thin gritty skin. Our meat
is the gelatinous type of meat. Our bones, pith.

A farmer holds out the *quenepas* as we pass him.
He holds his hands out on the road.
We pass him and another farmer reappears a mile up.
And we pass another and another.
The hands of farmers are gates.

This road is dust.
We must become green-feathered
Amazons circling the mountain
defying extinction.

CPSIA information can be obtained
at www.ICGtesting.com
Printed in the USA
BVOW08s2242210317
479130BV00001B/5/P

9 781597 097635